Admissions to Independent Elite Boarding & Day Schools and Ivy League & Stanford and MIT in the United States of America

Charlotte Elizabeth Courtenay

Copyright © 2024 by – Charlotte Elizabeth Courtenay – All Rights Reserved.

It is not legal to reproduce, duplicate, or transmit any part of this document in either electronic means or printed format. Recording of this publication is strictly prohibited.

Toll Free Calls: (US & Canada) 1-855-54-Elite (1-855-543-5483)
International Callers: 1-412-92-Elite (1-412-923-5483)

Email: Info@BoardingSchoolsIvyLeagueOxbridge.com

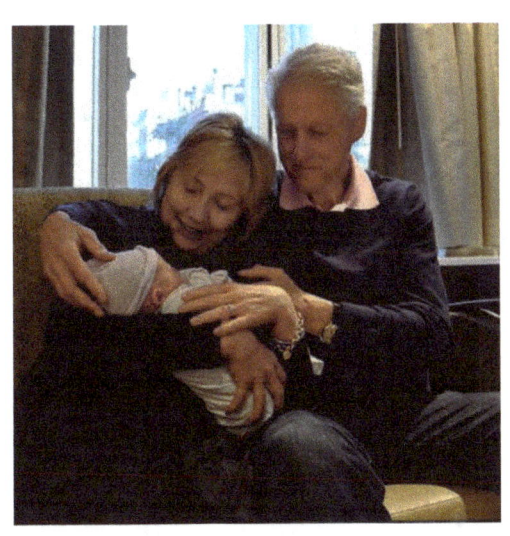

image tweeted by @BarackObama

Table of Contents

Dedication	i
Acknowledgment	ii
About the Author	iii
Foreword	1
USA Elite Boarding Schools and the Relationship Relevance to Ivy League and Stanford and MIT, and to other Elite Prestigious Colleges and Universities in Competitive University Admissions	2
Where to Begin	5
Summer Enrichment Pre-College Programs for Academically Gifted and Talented Youth	10
Things to consider when choosing a Boarding School and Pre-College Programs	11
Bonus: How to Get the Best Letters of Recommendation–Guaranteed!	15
There are two additional Primary Factors in the Admission Applications Process for Students applying to Graduate School or Professional School.	18
Bonus: Ace the Interview! Get Your Ivy League and or other Elite Prestigious College and University Offer!	18
A Final Note on the Admissions Process	21
Recommended Reading	26
Annual Calendar/Weekly Planner	27

Dedication

This First Edition of Admissions to Independent Elite Boarding & Day Schools and Ivy League & Stanford and MIT in the United States of America is dedicated to:

Our USA Presidents and our entire First Families and extended Family, Members of all Three Branches of Government who are Graduates of Boarding Schools, Ivy League and Stanford and MIT, other Elite Prestigious Colleges and Universities and Military Service Academies in our USA, including Oxbridge and St. Andrews and other Russell Group Universities in the UK.

My parents, Mary & James, my siblings, Bernard & Samantha.

The Sisters of St. Joseph De Cluny Nuns, world headquarters in Paris, France.

In the memory of my late husband Raymond Jr. Genius IQ 185 to 205 range. He encouraged me to write this book. Raymond sustained a traumatic brain injury in a traffic accident. He died of Covid 19 in 2021 during the worldwide pandemic.

In the memory of late world leaders:

President John F. Kennedy

Attorney General Robert F. Kennedy

President George H.W. Bush

Acknowledgment

My sincerest appreciation and gratitude to my dearest beloved father-in-law, Professor of Medicine Dr. G.A. Howard, for his encouragement and unwavering support in all my endeavors.

The conceptual framework for this admissions guidebook was written while I was a Graduate Student at the University of Oxford, England, in the United Kingdom. Then updated while working as a Deputy Warden in the largest Hall of Residence as well as Head of House named for the President, to Undergraduate and Graduate Students and Fellows at the University of St. Andrews, Scotland, in the United Kingdom. The framework updated again during a year post graduate research on Harvard campus in Cambridge Massachusetts.

This book was written during my time researching various types of Boarding Schools in the United Kingdom such as the 'Seven Original Public Schools,' and in the United States of America namely the 'The Eight Schools,' among other elite prestigious schools which collectively – historically are the 'Feeder Schools' to Oxbridge & St. Andrews and Ivy League & Stanford & MIT, other elect Russell Group Universities in the UK and other Prestigious Universities in the USA, including Military Service Academies in the UK & USA.

Many thanks to Project Manager Mr. James D., Account Manager Mr. Ryan H., Mr. Steve P., and the Editorial Team, the Book Cover Design Team, and the entire Team at Amazon Book Publications.

About the Author

The University of Oxford-Educated Social Scientist, Charlotte Courtenay, a New Times Best Seller, the sole proprietor of the International Consulting Company https://www.boardingschoolsivyleagueoxbridge.com, a Senior Education Consultant facilitating admission to top independent boarding and day schools and universities in the UK & USA, the most influential Political Strategist of our 21st Century, achieving political victories in elections for new and incumbent candidates for UK Prime Ministers, US Presidents and Vice Presidents, including the appointments of Cabinet Members and Supreme Court Justice Nominees, both Chambers of Congress, State Governors, G20 and OECD Heads of State, Heads of Multi-National Organizations, such as the Head of the UN and EU, G20 and leaders in countries and organizations such as the World Bank and IMF, University Chancellors & Presidents at institutions in our UK & USA and other leaders in countries and organizations around our world.

Foreword

In the United States United Kingdom, about 10% of all children 5-18 years attend independent schools, including 1% in the USA and 1% in the UK attending boarding schools, yet in both countries, 50% to 60% of all students at Ivy League and Stanford and MIT, Oxbridge and St Andrews, attended independent schools in general, elite prestigious boarding schools in particular. This means 90% of all the children in the United States and United Kingdom, are competing for only 40% to 50% of the admission spots available at Ivy League and Stanford and MIT, Oxbridge and St. Andrews. Students with aspirations of holding the highest offices of power - such as President of the USA, Members of Congress, Supreme Court Justices, Prime Minister of the UK, Members of Parliament, Heads of Countries and International Organizations, Ambassadors, Heads of Financial Sectors, Head of Corporations, Heads of Hospitals, Heads of International Legal Firms, Heads of elite prestigious schools, colleges, and universities, must have as a prerequisite one or more degrees from Ivy League and or Oxbridge. In most instances persons holding these positions are also a product of boarding schools.

USA Elite Boarding Schools and the Relationship Relevance to Ivy League and Stanford and MIT, and to other Elite Prestigious Colleges and Universities in Competitive University Admissions

Parents and young adult students alike, engage in the decision whether to choose boarding school, local independent day school, or local state school. The consideration in the biggest why to select boarding school: which ones are worth considering, the primary reason the overwhelming number of families make this crucial decision – the boarding school option.

There's indeed a formula to gaining admission to Ivy League and Stanford and MIT, and other elite prestigious Colleges and Universities in the United States of America as well as Military Service Academies, and in the UK to Oxbridge and St. Andrews and other Elite Russell Group Universities. Admission to this distinguished club does not happen by chance, this takes years of appropriate preparation, brilliant strategies, and effective planning.

Charlotte, on behalf of the Courtenay Company, known as Boarding Schools Ivy League and Oxbridge, prepared this document specifically for parents and students embarking on the best decision to move forward with the boarding school option. This is a short guidebook, thus, while I include the weblinks to the best boarding school options in each region and state to gain admission to particular Ivy League and selective colleges and universities, this document is not meant to be a complete list of all boarding school options in the United States, United Kingdom, Switzerland, Canada, France, or

Italy.

However, I do provide weblinks to view more complete lists of independent schools. Indeed, the reason for putting forward this short guidebook is that parents and students have a step-by-step concise reference to help families save valuable time and financial resources.

Let me get to the point. There are feeder pipelines Junior Boarding Preparatory Schools/Middle School grade/year 5-9 to Senior Secondary Boarding Preparatory High Schools grade/year 9-12, which are the primary feeder pipeline schools to the Ivy League and most selective Colleges and Universities in the United States. Gaining admission/membership into these most prestigious boarding schools is the guarantee of admission to Ivy League and or other most prestigious colleges and universities. Almost all the wealthy families in this country have legacies at our nation's most prestigious boarding schools, Ivy League and most prestigious colleges and universities. Indeed, over 50% of students past and present at our nation's most prestigious colleges and universities are the product of independent schools. Although currently there are slightly less than ten percent of students in the entire nation attending private schools, yet there's a private Prep School advantage to gaining admission to top colleges and universities, as such institutions of higher learning, consider students at Prep Schools much more prepared to be successful at top private and public research universities.

Preparation for life begins prior to our birth. Those who are graduates of elite boarding schools or graduates of an Ivy League or other elite prestigious college or university you might already know and understand how to navigate your children through this process. The aims and purpose of this document are that we at Boarding Schools, Ivy League and Oxbridge, desire for parents with or without a high school diploma or college/university degree, regardless of financial resources, to read and understand this document/guide framed with simplified language to help with the process to elite boarding school admissions and subsequently elite college and university admissions. We hope to create wider access to elite boarding schools for all families, thus creating wider access to Ivy League and the most elite prestigious colleges and universities for ALL students.

Here's how to help your children gain admission to the elite boarding schools of their choice, which will guarantee their admission to Ivy League and or other highly selective, elite prestigious colleges and universities. Are you intending to send your children to Junior Boarding Preparatory School for Middle School Grades 5–9? Parents wishing to send children to boarding schools prior to Middle School can purchase our UK version of this guidebook Admissions to Elite Independent Boarding & Day Schools and Oxbridge & St. Andrews in the United Kingdom. To review options for Preparatory Boarding Schools in the United Kingdom, which accepts boarding students in Year 2/age 7 years.

Parents need to plan carefully where you will raise your children from Pre-Kindergarten to Grade 4, whether you wish to send your children to US Junior Boarding Schools at Grade 5 at age 10 years. Parents need to research the quality of schools available locally–both private and public. Are there excellent private elementary/primary school options for ages 2 to 10 years? Are there high-quality public Magnet Gifted and Talented schools for elementary/primary school options for ages 2-10 years?

Where to Begin

The National Association of Independent Schools website (NAIS) can help you find Private Day and Boarding Schools for your children in Nursery/Early Years to Kindergarten (age 3 or 5 years) to Grade 12 (age 18 years) in every state. Please view the quick link to NAIS https://www.nais.org

Also, see a more comprehensive list of USA Boarding Schools by category here https://usboardingschools.com

First, select the best private school option for your children ages 2 or 3 years old to Grade 4 age 10 years in your local or nearby community. Get to know the names of the top three private schools in your County or Parish or Borough. Visit each school with your child at age 2 or 3 years old, then make your final decision to apply for admission. Consider the values, interests, and needs of your family. Then, select the best choice for your children based on your aspirations and goals for each individual child and for your entire family.

Towards the end of Grade 3, age 8 or 9 years–in the spring, take your children to visit a select number of Junior Preparatory Boarding Schools. Have your children spend a couple of weeks in summer programs at your top final choices. Then apply to those schools in the autumn/fall when your children are in Grade 4, age 9 years, for admission to start the first year of Middle School–Grade 5, age 9 or 10 years. Children have a 50 to 70% chance of admission acceptance rate to Junior/Preparatory Boarding Schools, which are the feeder schools for achieving matriculation to the most highly selective Senior Secondary Boarding Preparatory/High Schools.

To learn more about these schools for admission of Middle School students in Grades 5 to 9, please refer to the Junior Boarding Schools Association quick link https://www.jbsa.org Also, see a more complete list of USA Boarding Schools by category here https://usboardingschools.com

Junior Boarding Schools do an excellent job in preparing students for competitive results on the PSAT required for admission to the highly selective Senior Secondary Boarding High Schools.

In contrast, waiting to start the boarding school application process when your children are ready to enter Grade 9, age 14 years, to the highly selective Senior Secondary Boarding Preparatory High Schools application for admission process, students, in general, have only a 12 to 25% chance of admission to the top 10 most prestigious boarding schools. Students at Junior Boarding Schools, in particular, have a certainty of gaining admission to the highly selective Senior Secondary Boarding Preparatory High Schools. These world-renowned top Senior Boarding Schools are a guarantee that ALL students Will Gain Admission to our nation's Ivy League and or other most elite, highly selective prestigious colleges and universities. As aforementioned, over half of all the students at such higher education institutions are the product of private schools, boarding schools in particular, although less than 10% of all students in the USA attend private schools, and of that number, 1% attended boarding schools. In the United Kingdom, more children attend independent/private schools, and of that number, about 1% attend boarding schools. All pupils at these elite boarding schools in our USA gain entry to Ivy League and or other elite, highly prestigious Colleges and Universities in the United States, as well as Oxbridge and St. Andrews and or other elite prestigious colleges and universities in our USA and other elite Russell Group Colleges and Universities in the United Kingdom.

Senior Boarding Schools in the United States are as highly selective as Ivy League and elite highly selective prestigious colleges and universities.

The competition for a limited number of available places is very keen with so many applicants from the Junior Boarding Schools, from students in independent day schools, and students in local government schools across the United States, as well as prospective students from overseas - particularly from Asia and Europe.

Get ahead of the competition by getting your children admitted to feeder pipeline Junior Boarding Schools in the first instance for guaranteed acceptance to a top Senior Boarding Schools – the feeder pipeline to Ivy League and other elite prestigious colleges and universities.

To start reviewing Senior Boarding Schools, begin with the top ten most competitive and prestigious Senior Boarding Preparatory Schools in the US. Here's the quick link to the Eight Schools Association http://www.8schools.org Here's the link to the ten Schools Organization http://www.tenschools.org Senior Boarding Schools do an excellent job in preparing students with rigorous Honors and Advance Placement courses, to take the ACT and SAT Examinations for the competitive admissions process to Ivy League and other elite highly selective prestigious colleges and universities.

To review a broader list of Boarding Schools, which starts from Grades 6 to 12 and Senior Preparatory Boarding Schools, which starts from Grades 9–12, in some instances, Grades 8-12. These elite prestigious boarding schools are overwhelmingly located in New

England in particular, the North-East and Mid-Atlantic States in general. Boarding Schools, in general, in all parts of the United States are considered relatively very good.

Please refer to the comprehensive list of boarding schools in the US via these links herein. Select your Country of choice: USA, UK, Switzerland, Canada, France, Italy. Then select your Region, State/Province of Religious Denomination of preference please click on advance search.

Quick link to New England USA Boarding Schools
https://www.boardingschools.com

Quick link to North-East USA Boarding Schools
https://www.boardingschools.com

Quick link to Mid-Atlantic USA Boarding Schools
https://www.boardingschools.com

Quick link to Mid-West USA Boarding Schools
https://www.boardingschools.com

Quick link to South-East USA Boarding Schools
https://www.boardingschools.com

Quick link to South-West USA Boarding Schools
https://www.boardingschools.com

Quick link to West USA Boarding Schools
https://www.boardingschools.com

Quick link to USA Roman Catholic Boarding Schools
https://www.boardingschoolreview.com/catholic-boarding-schools-religion

Quick link to USA Episcopal Boarding Schools
https://usboardingschools.com/episcopal

Quick link to USA Sports Boarding Schools
http://www.boardingschoolreview.com/boarding-schools-by-sport

Quick link to USA Extra Curricula Boarding Schools
https://www.boardingschoolreview.com/boarding-schools-by-extracurricular

Quick link to USA Arts Boarding Schools
https://www.boardingschoolreview.com/arts-boarding-schools

Summer Enrichment Pre-College Programs for Academically Gifted and Talented Youth

Harvard University Pre-College Programs
http://www.summer.harvard.edu

Stanford University Pre-College Programs
https://summerinstitutes.spcs.stanford.edu

Yale University Pre-College Programs
https://summer.yale.edu

Columbia University Pre-College Programs
http://sps.columbia.edu

Princeton University Pre-College Programs
https://www.giftedstudy.org

Duke University Pre-College Programs
https://tip.duke.edu

Notre Dame University Pre-College Programs
https://precollege.nd.edu

John Hopkins Pre-College Programs
https://cty.jhu.edu

Georgetown University Pre-College Programs
https://summer.georgetown.edu/all-programs

Vanderbilt University Pre-College Programs
https://pty.vanderbilt.edu

Emory University
http://precollege.emory.edu

Things to consider when choosing a Boarding School and Pre-College Programs

History of the Institution – Read the founding history, including the list of Notable Alumni. Who's at the table? Former Notable Alumni as well as current students who will in the future chart courses of their own and no doubt will someday be added to the list of Notable Alumni. Notable Alumni whom you have never met are present at the table at all these institutions. Their achievements are also your shared history and legacy. Becoming a member of a world-renowned prestigious institution, you have membership in the same club of notables. Like members of our world-renown secret societies.

Review the list of The World's Most Elite Boarding Schools to select the best schools in the US, UK, Switzerland, Canada, France, Italy. https://www.boardingschools.com

List of G20 Schools: https://en.wikipedia.org/wiki/G20_Schools

Resources. Cadre–what is the Education Level of the Faculty. What schools and colleges and universities they've attended. The Library/Media Center, STEM: Science Labs and Computer Labs, and other Learning Centers like on-site Museums and Observatories.

Endowment of the Institution. The sustainability of the school/college or university as well as for Financial Aid Bursaries for current and future students. Is the admission policy 'need-blind' - meaning whether admission decisions are made based solely on perspective students' academic merit gifts and talents, without regard to applicants' ability to pay fees.

Matriculation/Destinations of School Leavers at Junior Boarding Schools to Senior Boarding Schools.

Matriculation Destinations of School Leavers at Senior Boarding Schools to Ivy League and other elite prestigious colleges and universities in the USA, Oxbridge and St. Andrews and other Russell Group Colleges and Universities in the UK, and other prestigious International Colleges and Universities.

Elite Club Membership. When you arrive at your Ivy League and or Prestigious College or University, you are already a member of an elite club, your particular boarding school, and having attended boarding school in general.

Proximity to others with Power and Wealth. Students make and build good network connections with others for Professional Networking - prior to, during, and after college or university. The adage who you know is as important as what you know rings true for graduates of these elite institutions. The Elite Club Boarding School Graduates, Ivy League and other Elite Prestigious Colleges/Universities are pervasive in our Nation's Capital–Washington DC at the Federal Level–in all Three Branches of Government, in the White House, Capitol Hill - Congress and the Supreme Court, New York City's Financial District - especially Wall Street. When interviewing for dream career roles, chances are the panel will likely be made up of graduates from elite Boarding and Day and Public Boarding Schools, certainly Ivy League and elite prestigious Private and Public Ivy League Colleges and Universities, including Military Academies.

[List of presidents of the United States by education](#)

Parents may decide to keep their K-12 children close to home at Prestigious Independent Day Schools, Public State Quality Schools - such as Public Magnet Schools for Gifted and Talented Students and Prestigious State Governor's Public Boarding Schools for the highly gifted students demonstrating the most academic promise. Get your children's IQ tested at no cost by your local School District Psychologist to qualify for Gifted and Talented Services. Children need to score at least a 130 IQ to qualify for Gifted and Talented Education Matrix of Services.

Parents can also supplement your children's education in selecting a wealth of summer programs to help develop your children's academic curiosity gifts and talents at Middle/Junior Boarding Schools, Secondary/High Boarding Schools and at Colleges and Universities offering Pre-College Programs. Please note that the highest-paid compensation State/Public School Teachers are in New York, Connecticut, California, Massachusetts, and New Jersey. The public education in affluent catchment areas of several school districts in these states are on par with the best Independent Day Schools. Several Public Schools in these states have a solid record of sending graduates to Ivy League Colleges and Universities and other prestigious colleges and universities.

Day School Students in Elementary/Primary & Middle School Years/Grade 2 at age 7 years to Grade 6 at age 11 years, can choose Boarding Schools as a Summer Enrichment refer to website lists of schools above. Parents should focus on your children's areas of interest or on areas where your children need more developmental support, English and other Modern Languages, STEM–Science, Technology, Engineering and Mathematics. Music – there are great options in London and Vienna to improve their skills on their instruments as well as The Julliard School https://www.julliard.edu in New York USA. Academic including specialty study activities and opportunities, such as Pilot Training only 1:15hr to the field trip venues in Washington DC at Randoph Macon Academy in Front Royal Virginia https://www.rma.edu America's only full time High-School Flight Program, where students in Grade 6-12 starting at age 11 years, learn to fly airplanes before they learn to drive cars! Athletics – Equestrian activities, improve their Golf or Tennis at the US top Sports Academy in the World https://www.imgacademy.com/boarding-school

Day School Students in High School Years/Grades 7–12 & PG Boarding Schools as a Summer Enrichment (refer to website lists of schools above) Ivy League and Elite Colleges and Universities as a Pre-College Summer Enrichment (refer to website lists of schools above or do an advance narrower or wider search for other colleges and universities with Pre-College Programs, also refer to our UK version of this guide titled Admissions to Independent Elite Boarding & Day Schools and Oxbridge and St. Andrews in the United Kingdom). Students take summer courses in residence at Ivy League and Elite Colleges and Universities in the US, or at Oxbridge and St. Andrews and other Russell Group Elite Colleges and Universities in the UK, so that they gain experience with more rigorous college-level courses at prestigious institutions of higher learning with highly academically competitive and motivated like-minded peers to prepare for highly selective college/university admissions process.

Bonus: How to Get the Best Letters of Recommendation–Guaranteed!

1. The Highest ACT and SAT Scores

2. The Highest High School GPA–the Rigor of the School and AP Courses taken are Important

3. A. Winning Personal Statement Essay

4. The Best Letters of Recommendation–Expert Testimony

5. Some Elite Prestigious Colleges and Universities also require an in-Person Interview. The Interview is at the heart of Oxbridge and some Russell Group Admissions– or those interested in applying to Colleges and Universities in the UK.

How students should go about the business of obtaining the Best Letters of Recommendation/Expert Testimony:

1. Ask your Three Top High School Teachers/Three Top Professors for Undergraduates applying to Graduate Programs. The Teachers/Professors selected to write your winning letters of recommendation should be those whom you're impressed upon with your academic scholarship and other gifts and talents.

2. Ask two of the Teachers/Professors each to write a letter supporting your application to the list of various Ivy League and other elite prestigious colleges and universities. Tell them why the letters are so important to your aspirations and career goals. Tell them why you chose them to support your applications (such as Chair of Department or Academic Dean or Principal–the higher the rank of the teacher/professor, the more weight is given to the letter of recommendation by the admissions committee at your desired higher

education institutions), of all your other teachers/professors whom you could choose to do the honor. Make certain to tell each of them that you've discussed the matter and the rationale for your referee choices with your parents.

3. Ask one of the three Teachers/Professors you selected to write your Winning Letters of Recommendation to write you a letter with more Expert Testimony of Seven other Teachers/Professors and Administrators. This Teacher/Professor must hold you in high regard in order to agree to take on this Research Paper Letter of Recommendation. Approach Seven (additional) Teachers/Professors and administrators–ask each of them to write you a letter of Recommendation to your chosen Ivy League and other elite prestigious colleges and universities. Ask them to give their sealed letters to that very Special Teacher/Professor whom you've selected to write the third letter of recommendation. Inform the Third Referee of the names of the seven other Teachers/Professors who will give to him or her the letters of recommendation in seal envelopes. Tell the Third Referee that you need him or her to open those seven letters and cite quotations from each of those seven letters in the brilliant winning letter of recommendation/expert testimony that he or she will write in support of your application to each of your desired list of Ivy League and other elite prestigious colleges and universities. That Genius Letter of Recommendation includes the expert testimony of Eight Educators: the Writer–the Third Referee, as well as Seven Teachers/Professors and Administrators. That letter will put your admission application in serious contention for a place at each of your desired higher education choices. Indeed, your application will impress upon the Admission Committee at each institution. After all, ten Teachers/Professors and Administrators at your current Educational Institution have spoken on your behalf. Although only

three letters were requested, your brilliance in obtaining the expert testimony of Ten Educators will make a lasting impression in the highly competitive admission selection process. The Selection Committee at each higher education institution will have a difficult time declining your application for admission. Admissions Committees do not wish to say no to the hearts and minds of Ten Educators. They would much rather reach a consensus with an affirmative nod to your application for admission.

4. The Secondary Factors of the Admission Application include but are not limited to aspects like extra-curricular–Leadership Ability such as Speech and Debate, Arts–Music and Drama, Sports, Legacy of Parents and other Family/Relatives, and Demographics–for Diversity among the Student Body (except at Oxbridge & St. Andrews and other Elite Russell Group Colleges and Universities, among other factors, where only ability to succeed in chosen academic subject/degree is taken into consideration. Refer to our publication on Admissions to Elite Boarding and Day Schools and Oxbridge & St. Andrews in the United Kingdom.)

There are two additional Primary Factors in the Admission Applications Process for Students applying to Graduate School or Professional School.

1. The two Research Papers/Academic Writing Samples–the higher education institutions are interested in your ability to write and conduct independent research at the Graduate level.

2. Resume/Curriculum Vita–the higher education institutions are interested in knowing how you made good use of your time during summer vacation periods during your Undergraduate years–such as Study abroad, Internships, and others

Bonus: Ace the Interview! Get Your Ivy League and or other Elite Prestigious College and University Offer!

Start doing your research the moment you decide to apply to a college or university that requires an interview as part of the application for admission. Prepare for the possible questions you might be asked and how you will respond, demonstrating your intelligence.

Think of who you are now and who you desire to become in your future career.

Think of what you have accomplished already and what you desire to accomplish in the future. Think of a time when you and your family and your teachers were proud of your achievements.

Think of where you are now, where you desire to attend college/university, and where you desire to practice your career.

Think why you're a high achiever, why you desire your intended higher education Course of Study, and why you're applying to particular colleges and universities.

Think about how you've achieved your current level of success and how your desired colleges and universities will help you to develop and sustain your future success.

Get to know as much as you can about your desired college/university in general and in particular about the research interests/publications of the Academic Scholars in your department of chosen Course of Study–major and minor concentrations.

What do you want to learn and gain from admission to study at your top chosen college/university?

There's no greater cardinal sin than applicants who show up for an interview without any serious prior knowledge of the institution in general and, worst yet, of the research interests of the Academics in your chosen intended field of study. Please do not make this common mistake. Go on the websites of the colleges and universities and learn as much as you can about the Professors, learn their titles, their peer-reviewed Scholarly Journal Articles and their books and book chapters. Start a conversation with those you're interested in having as your Academic Advisor/Dissertation Chair/Supervisor. Email them with thoughtfully framed queries.

Demonstrate with your responses how your research interests align with the work of the academic department via mentioning publication works of current Academics in the department as well as Emeritus Academics. Also, mention the publications of Academics in other comparatively elite prestigious colleges and universities whose research is similar and with whom some of the Academics you're interviewing may have co-published. This presents you as highly intelligent, your regard for persons with similar research interests to your own, thus you do not appear merely to be making attempts to impress the Academics with whom you're currently interviewing, but rather showing that you have wider knowledge of yours and their research interests with knowledge of the leading Scholars in your chosen academic field of study. This also implies that you're interested in Graduate School studies, developing within your chosen field with their guidance. They will want to choose you before you have an opportunity to interview with the Academics in the other colleges and universities you're mentioned. Academics like students who're applying not only for the 'name' of the college/university but that the decision to apply is also based in part on the Scholarship of the Professors who will be engaged in your teaching and learning development as you advance and make progress towards your chosen career. This will set you apart, putting your application in contention as a serious candidate for admission to your top choice college/university.

A Final Note on the Admissions Process

Admissions Officers compare students' Standardized Tests Scores, as well as the Academic Rigor of the schools attended by the applicant's seeking admission to their elite, prestigious institutions. Their decisions are often based on 'The Like Me Syndrome' applicants most similar to their own educational backgrounds. Who are the Admissions Officers at highly selective boarding schools? They are most often graduates of highly selective boarding schools. Who are the Admissions Officers at Ivy League and Oxbridge? They are most often graduates of Ivy League and Stanford and MIT, Oxbridge and St. Andrews and other elite prestigious colleges and universities in the US and UK. Hence Admissions Officers consciously or unconsciously admit/make more than half the admissions offers to applicants with proximity to their own personal educational experiences. This preference is known as 'Signaling' – choosing applicants from the 'Power Elite' – known collectively as 'Prestige Schools.' This crosses over into every aspect of social organization and culture with regard to education and employment. The White House and Congress – Capitol Hill and the Supreme Court, New York's Financial District – Wall Street, are filled with Ivy League and Oxbridge and Russell Group Graduates, and this is the case of Prestige School graduates in every country in our world. Admissions Officers are 'People with Power,' and people with power are beholden to other 'People with Power.' Membership to the Power Elite starts with Membership at highly selective World Renown Boarding Prestige Schools in the US and UK, - the Golden Ticket to Membership to Ivy League and other elite prestigious colleges and universities in the US, Oxbridge and St. Andrews, and other Russell Group elite prestigious Colleges and Universities in the UK.

The Prudence of our Platinum Individualized Consulting Service can help your family navigate the process of choosing the right school for your children. At Boarding Schools Ivy League and Oxbridge, we have a 'Need Blind Policy,' and as such we seek only quality students whom with can support in the application process to Boarding Schools, Ivy League, and Oxbridge, and other elite and prestigious schools and colleges and universities, without regard to students and family's ability to pay us consulting fees. Complete the General Inquiry Form on
https://www.boardingschoolsivyleagueoxbridge.com

If you would like to be considered for reduced consulting fees, please also complete the application through FACTS: https://online.factsmgt.com/signin/4M3CT

The assessment report we receive from FACTS gives us a recommendation in determining the amount of your fee remission/consulting fees for each student, and or tutoring fees for each child. All Boarding Schools in the US offer financial aid; some have 'need-blind admission policies.' All colleges and universities in the US offer Financial Aid, and some have 'need-blind admission policies.' Only the most prestigious schools and colleges and universities have 'Need Blind Policy' - meaning the decision to offer admission to students is based entirely on academic merit and other gifts and talents without any knowledge of family finances, irrespective of whether students and their families can afford to pay tuition and room and board fees.

There are scholarships for non/EU students to help afford the overseas fees at UK colleges and universities, such as the Overseas Research Student Scholarship known as the ORS, which reduces the overseas students rate to the Home/EU Rate. Overseas/non-EU residents pay a higher rate. There are scholarships for non-EU students to help afford the overseas fees, such as the Overseas Research Student Scholarship known as the ORS which reduces the overseas students' rate to the Home/EU Rate. Also, the Rhodes Scholarship to Oxford, the Clarendon Scholarship at Oxford, and the Gates Scholarship to Cambridge. US Students can also apply for the Fulbright Scholarship, the Marshall Scholarship, your local Rotary Club and more. Ask the departments at the schools, colleges, and universities where you're applying for a list of scholarships with details on how to apply for those scholarships. Please do not let the ability to pay discourage you from choosing to apply for the best educational opportunities for your children.

We look forward to reviewing your children's application/s for Platinum Consulting Services. We receive many more applications than we can accept; however, we endeavor to select the children with the most academic promise for success at Boarding Schools, Ivy League, and other elite prestigious colleges and universities. In the event that you're offered a spot with one of our Platinum Consultants, we look forward to guiding you and your children through this enrichment process. In the event that we are oversubscribed and without any available Platinum Consulting spots, then we recommend that you consider A Telethon Consultation Appointment with our President to help steer you in the right direction of Boarding or Day School and college or university choice. Indeed, it is amazing how much knowledge on this process you can acquire and gain in a ten-minute conversation. Please note that our President specializes in Platinum Consulting in the following areas: Admissions to Oxbridge and elite prestigious Russell Group Colleges and Universities, Admissions to Boarding Schools USA & UK & Switzerland, General Ivy League Admissions Knowledge and Process, in Particular–Ivy

League Non-Traditional/Alternative Admissions Process–such as Adult Continuing Education for Bachelors and Master's Degrees in Evening and Online Programs at Ivy League and other elite prestigious colleges and universities.

At Boarding Schools, Ivy League and Oxbridge, we hope that parents and students alike find this guidebook easy to read and a good resource for selecting the best local Elementary/Primary Private Day Schools or Public Magnet/Gifted and Talented Schools in your City, County or State, the best Junior/Middle Boarding and Day Schools, Senior/High Boarding and Day Schools, and Pre-College Programs, to take you to your ultimate Undergraduate and subsequently Graduate and Professional Schools. Also, for those wishing to study abroad, get our UK version of this guidebook on Admissions to Elite Independent Boarding & Day Schools and Oxbridge & St. Andrews in the United Kingdom Boarding and Day Schools Oxbridge and Elite Russell Group Colleges and Universities. The Golden Ticket to Ivy League and Elite Colleges and Universities in the USA, as well as Oxbridge and St. Andrews, elite prestigious Russell Group Colleges and Universities in the United Kingdom are at the heart of boarding schools.

We wish you the very best with all your endeavors from Kindergarten to Grade 12, Undergraduate, Graduate and Professional Studies, and in your chosen career. In the event that parents and students would like additional assistance in selecting the best Day Schools, Boarding Schools, and Summer Programs in the US, UK, and Switzerland, please complete the General Inquiry Form on the Contact Page of our website.

Remember: All schools and all grades are not considered equal. Schools and Grades are stratified – based on the type of educational institution and the faculty assigning the grades to students' assignments/work products.

https://www.boardingschoolsivyleagueoxbridge.com

Recommended Reading

Preparing for Power: *America's Elite Boarding Schools.*

Four Centuries after this publication, the same schools in the USA have a significant number of students each year matriculating at Ivy League and Stanford and MIT and other elite prestigious Colleges and Universities.

Harvard Crimson

The Harvard Crimson

Forbes University Rankings

US News & World Report

Annual Calendar/Weekly Planner

August

1	2	3	4	5	6	7
8	9	10	11	12	13	14
15	16	17	18	19	20	21
22	23	24	25	26	27	28
29	30	31				

August
First Week

Second Week

August
Third Week

Fourth Week

September

1	2	3	4	5	6	7
8	9	10	11	12	13	14
15	16	17	18	19	20	21
22	23	24	25	26	27	28
29	30					

September
First Week

Second Week

September
Third Week

Fourth Week

October

1	2	3	4	5	6	7	
8	9	10	11	12	13	14	
15	16	17	18	19	20	21	
22	23	24	25	26	27	28	
29	30	31					

October

First Week

Second Week

October

Third Week

Fourth Week

November

1	2	3	4	5	6	7
8	9	10	11	12	13	14
15	16	17	18	19	20	21
22	23	24	25	26	27	28
29	30					

November

First Week

Second Week

November
Third Week

Fourth Week

December

1	2	3	4	5	6	7
8	9	10	11	12	13	14
15	16	17	18	19	20	21
22	23	24	25	26	27	28
29	30	31				

December

First Week

Second Week

December

Third Week

Fourth Week

January

1	2	3	4	5	6	7
8	9	10	11	12	13	14
15	16	17	18	19	20	21
22	23	24	25	26	27	28
29	30	31				

January
First Week

Second Week

January
Third Week

Fourth Week

February

1	2	3	4	5	6	7
8	9	10	11	12	13	14
15	16	17	18	19	20	21
22	23	24	25	26	27	28
29						

February
First Week

Second Week

February
Third Week

Fourth Week

March

1	2	3	4	5	6	7
8	9	10	11	12	13	14
15	16	17	18	19	20	21
22	23	24	25	26	27	28
29	30	31				

March
First Week

Second Week

March
Third Week

Fourth Week

April

1	2	3	4	5	6	7
8	9	10	11	12	13	14
15	16	17	18	19	20	21
22	23	24	25	26	27	28
29	30					

April

First Week

Second Week

April
Third Week

Fourth Week

May

1	2	3	4	5	6	7
8	9	10	11	12	13	14
15	16	17	18	19	20	21
22	23	24	25	26	27	28
29	30	31				

May
First Week

Second Week

May
Third Week

Fourth Week

June

1	2	3	4	5	6	7
8	9	10	11	12	13	14
15	16	17	18	19	20	21
22	23	24	25	26	27	28
29	30					

June

First Week

Second Week

June
Third Week

Fourth Week

July

1	2	3	4	5	6	7
8	9	10	11	12	13	14
15	16	17	18	19	20	21
22	23	24	25	26	27	28
29	30	31				

July

First Week

Second Week

July
Third Week

Fourth Week

www.ingramcontent.com/pod-product-compliance
Lightning Source LLC
Chambersburg PA
CBHW041148110526
44590CB00027B/4167